Garden Time

Also by W.S. Merwin

W.S. MERWIN

Garden Time

COPPER CANYON PRESS

Port Townsend, Washington

Cover art: Gwen Arkin, *The Garden House*

Endpapers and back cover art: © Sarah Cavanaugh, *Palm #3, Under the Lanai,*
2009. First published in *Narrative* Magazine in 2014.

Copper Canyon Press is in residence at Fort Worden State Park in
Port Townsend, Washington, under the auspices of Centrum. Centrum
is a gathering place for artists and creative thinkers from around the
world, students of all ages and backgrounds, and audiences seeking
extraordinary cultural enrichment.

LIBRARY OF CONGRESS CATALOGING-IN-PUBLICATION DATA

Names: Merwin, W. S. (William Stanley), 1927– author.
Title: Garden time / W.S. Merwin.
Description: Port Townsend, Washington : Copper Canyon Press, [2016]
Identifiers: LCCN 2015040767 | ISBN 9781556594991 (alk. paper)
Classification: LCC PS3563.E75 A6 2016 | DDC 811/.54 — dc23
LC record available at http://lccn.loc.gov/2015040767

3 5 7 9 8 6 4 2

Copper Canyon Press
Post Office Box 271
Port Townsend, Washington 98368

www.coppercanyonpress.org

To Paula

The hours of folly are measur'd by the clock,
but of wisdom: no clock can measure.

WILLIAM BLAKE, "PROVERBS OF HELL," FROM
THE MARRIAGE OF HEAVEN AND HELL

CONTENTS

Garden Time

THE MORNING

Would I love it this way if it could last
would I love it this way if it
were the whole sky the one heaven
or if I could believe that it belonged to me
a possession that was mine alone
or if I imagined that it noticed me
recognized me and may have come to see me
out of all the mornings that I never knew
and all those that I have forgotten
would I love it this way if I were somewhere else
or if I were younger for the first time
or if these very birds were not singing
or I could not hear them or see their trees
would I love it this way if I were in pain
red torment of body or gray void of grief
would I love it this way if I knew
that I would remember anything that is
here now anything anything

MY OTHER DARK

Sometimes in the dark I find myself
in a place that I seem to have known
in another time
and I wonder
whether it has changed through
sunrises and sunsets that I never saw
whether the things that I remember
are still there where I remember them
would I know them even if my hand
touched them in this present darkness
would they know me and have they been
waiting for me all this time
in the dark

NOT EARLY OR LATE

Is it I who have come to this age
or is it the age that has come to me
which one has brought along all these
silent images on their shadowy river
appearing and going away as the river does
all without a word though they all know me
I can see that they always knew where to find me
bringing me what they know I will recognize
what they know only I will recognize
to show me what I could not have seen before
then leave me to make sense of my own questions
going away making no promises

THE SCARAB QUESTIONS

Out of full shadow your sound emerges
at the end of the last morning in May
as we call the days on our calendars
but where did you begin without numbers
where did you come from this late morning
what do you remember as you ride your one note
on its dark sunbeam out into the daylight
your note is the time of your radiance
arriving once just as the sun does
but where were you before now where did you
come from before you were today

FROM OUR SHADOWS

There are so many words for sadness
and for joy so few
maybe none
that can tell
the sound of that secret spring
welling up from before words
though when its voice rises
within us
we want to be able to tell
someone about it
if they will stay to hear
talk about
what is beyond words
sadness can rise in us
in the midst of happiness
and joy can take us by surprise
in the midst of great sadness
both of them know us
from before we were here
but if we speak to them
only sadness lingers
to hear us out
joy disappears
to wait for us it may be
where we least expect it

O SILENT HANDS

Hands born of silence hands of silence
hands born of darkness hands of darkness
left hand of silence right hand of silence
hands of darkness in clear daylight
fingers of fire without sound or brightness
silent hands that bring music to pass
and it goes on echoing day and night
silent fingers' touch on the strings
or on the white keys that have no song of their own
finger ends commanding the dark openings in the flute
as it takes up its song of distance
the music touches the waiting darkness of the heart
touches it once and without recognizing it
and the silent heart welcomes the song home

THE SOUND OF IT

The rain stopped
you never hear it stop
then the dripping from the trees and then
how could anyone hear it not falling
not arriving and then
not arriving
other things must be happening that way
unheard all around us
you never hear the dog stop barking
whether you are listening or not
we hear things start up and go on
calling and shrieking and singing
saying hello saying good-bye but not
stopping
is that the way it is
is there no sound of stopping
and no sound to
the stopping of stopping
then no sound
without stopping

BLACK CHERRIES

Late in May as the light lengthens
toward summer the young goldfinches
flutter down through the day for the first time
to find themselves among fallen petals
cradling their day's colors in the day's shadows
of the garden beside the old house
after a cold spring with no rain
not a sound comes from the empty village
as I stand eating the black cherries
from the loaded branches above me
saying to myself Remember this

MORNING NEAR THE END OF MAY

Yesterday they mowed the long field
below the house out to the rim of oaks
and ash trees where the oriole sings again
over the valley and this still morning
the combed rows running the full length of it
flow on through sleep into the edge of dawn
through which the ghosts go home wading the bread
of mown grass along the unwaking rows
the ghosts go in under the walnut trees
older than anyone I remember
they were standing there long before I was born
and now as the daylight fills the hollow rows
the old trees gather the shadow under themselves
to guard all day for the dark queen

REMEMBERING SUMMER

Being too warm the old lady said to me
is better than being too cold I think now
in between is the best because you never
give it a thought but it goes by too fast
I remember the winter how cold it got
I could never get warm wherever I was
but I don't remember the summer heat like that
only the long days the breathing of the trees
the evenings with the hens still talking in the lane
and the light getting longer in the valley
the sound of a bell from down there somewhere
I can sit here now still listening to it

DAYLIGHT AFTER THE AUTUMN EQUINOX

Brightness plays high in the morning trees
time is nothing but its playing
it stops and holds still at its height
and the birds stop with it and stay silent
it will never be known how long that lasts
then the doves wake again in another age
the white footprints in the long fronds
begin their slow dance with the footprints of shadows
and the dancers move in the arms of shadows
that are silently celebrating the equinox
celebrating the going of the brightness
the remembered days of the long summer

TO THESE EYES

The only ones
I ever knew
you that have shown me
what I came to see
from the beginning
just as it was leaving
you that showed me the faces
in the realms of summer
the rivers the moments of gardens
all the roads that led here
the smiles of recognition
the silent rooms at nightfall
and have looked through the glasses
my mother was wearing when she died
you that I have never seen
except in a mirror
please go on showing me
faces you led me to
daylight the bird moment
the leaves of morning
as long as I look
hoping to catch sight
of what has not yet been seen

ONCE LATER

It is not until later
that you have to be young

it is one of the things
you meant to do later

but by then there is
someone else living there

with the shades rolled down
how could you have been young there

at that time
with all that was expected

then what happened to
the expectations

there is no sign of them there
a shadow passes across the window shade

what do they know in there
whoever they are

One at a time the drops find their own leaves
then others follow as the story spreads
they arrive unseen among the waking doves
who answer from the sleep of the valley
there is no other voice or other time

SUMMER SKY

July with sun-filled leaves drifting among the butterflies
I have been coming to this morning light since the day I was born
I saw its childhood as I sat alone in silence by the high window
no one else saw it no one else would ever recognize it
it is the same child now who watches the clouds change
they appear from out of sight and change as the moment passes through them

THE WINGS OF DAYLIGHT

Brightness appears showing us everything
it reveals the splendors it calls everything
but shows it to each of us alone
and only once and only to look at
not to touch or hold in our shadows
what we see is never what we touch
what we take turns out to be something else
what we see that one time departs untouched
while other shadows gather around us
the world's shadows mingle with our own
we had forgotten them but they know us
they remember us as we always were
they were at home here before the first came
everything will leave us except the shadows
but the shadows carry the whole story
at first daybreak they open their long wings

AFTER THE DRAGONFLIES

Dragonflies were as common as sunlight
hovering in their own days
backward forward and sideways
as though they were memory
now there are grown-ups hurrying
who never saw one
and do not know what they
are not seeing
the veins in a dragonfly's wings
were made of light
the veins in the leaves knew them
and the flowing rivers
the dragonflies came out of the color of water
knowing their own way
when we appeared in their eyes
we were strangers
they took their light with them when they went
there will be no one to remember us

FOREIGN ACCENTS

The words have been used for
so many things
how can they speak now
of this morning light
white on the pleated fronds
and the raucous talk of the mynahs
foreign here
as I am
at home here as I am
old as I am
with another memory
of the same place
the mynahs keep flying
around and around
disagreeing
What do we recognize

PORTENTS

A cherished machete
companion of twenty years
lies somewhere not far away
lost
marking the end of an age

you looked for it with me
but found no one

then came the dream
the old friend newly dead
asking for a book
I had on a high shelf
and when I climbed there
he took away the ladder
and lay on the floor laughing
at how little I knew
then he became a dark river

by day the known world
lost color
my hold on it felt loose
I imagine that was part
of the grief I knew

by then in the dusk
two redstarts
close together before winter
lit on a plum twig
near my hand
and stayed to watch me

VARIATIONS TO THE
ACCOMPANIMENT OF A CLOUD

Because I do not hope ever again
to pass this way I sing these
notes now in silence
each in its own time
one morning near the end of spring
among the invisible unheard stars I sing
this one time with the hope that is here
in every breath
may these notes be heard another morning
in another life
in another spring together

Because I do not hope ever to pass
this way again
one morning late in spring
in the cold rain above the valley I sing
in the old house I came to in my youth
on the ridge looking over the river
a house that had been left to its own silence
for half a century
home for bats and swallows and patches
of sunlight wandering across the floors
under holes in the roof on the day
I first saw it

and recognized it without knowing it
above the same river

Because I do not hope to see again
this spring morning with its cloud of light
that wakes the blackbird in the trees downhill
from the house I came to long ago
when I was young and the silence
was a summer day
that first summer that I would see
from these windows
I came to see
the plum trees flowering on the slope below
the snow swirling outside the kitchen
I will not see this morning fill
with light again along the green field
under the walnut trees those silent ancients
I reach out to it with words
it never hears

*Because I do not hope ever to find
my way again* to the moments of pure
single fortune and the unrepeated mistakes
that led me here

I look back in wonder
at how I found you and we came to be here
where has it gone
never was there one step backward

Although I do not hope to know again
what I have known since the beginning
not for a moment has it left me
I keep looking for what has always been mine
searching for it even as I
think of leaving it
my love was always
woven with leaving
moment by moment leaving
the one time

RIVER

Li Po the little boat is gone
that carried you ten thousand *li*
downstream past the gibbons calling
all the way from both banks and they
too are gone and the forests they
were calling from and you are gone
and every sound you heard is gone
now there is only the river
that was always on its own way

LOSS

Loss was my brother
is my brother
but I have no image of him

his name which was never used
was Hanson
it had been the name
of my mother's father
who had died as a young man

her child had been taken away
from my mother before
she ever saw him

to be bathed I suppose

they came and told her
that he was perfect in every way
and said they had never
seen such a beautiful child
and then they told her that he was dead

she sustained herself by believing
that he must have been dropped

somewhere just out of her sight
and out of her reach
and had fallen out of his empty name

all my life he has been near me
but I cannot tell you anything
about him

MORRIS GRAVES'S *BLIND BIRD*

This is the only way we can understand each other now
this is the only way I can listen to you
with our feet tangled in the white yarn bushes
known as the world

this is the way the holders of the blinding pins
came to be unable ever to hear
Hardy told me that he had seen an ancestor of yours
long ago when I was in the dark before I was born here

and I learned later that those with the pins
became unable to hear you when you kept singing
to yourself and your clear voice kept rising
out of the chords and great chorus of your ancestors

now as I listen to you I hear in your voice
the forgotten freedom leaping over the rocks
and flying flying again and the rocks are singing
under you out of the unending silence
where the world goes on beginning

THE MAPMAKER

Vermeer's geographer goes on looking
out of the window at a world that he
alone sees while in the room around him
the light has not moved as the centuries
have revolved in silence behind their clouds
beyond the leaves the seasons the numbers
he has not seen them out of that window
the world he sees is there as we see him
looking out at the light there in the window

BREAKFAST CUP

Here once more is the world of porcelain
distant but familiar like the morning
a land that does not know what it contains
with a language that was never spoken
and a white sky that has forgotten sound
a motionless place where someone stares out
from a bridge over no water flowing
and behind him someone bearing on one
shoulder a sack the same blue as his hair
pauses in mid-stride as he always did
and will do now for the rest of his life
someone else peers out of an empty house
at a world of changeless reassurance
that does not know us or forget us

EARLY ONE MORNING

Here is Memory walking in the dark
there are no pictures of her as she is
the coming day was never seen before
the stars have gone into another life
the dreams have left with no sound of farewell
insects wake flying up with their feet wet
trying to take the night along with them
Memory alone is awake with me
knowing that this may be the only time

THE LAUGHING CHILD

When she looked down from the kitchen window
into the back yard and the brown wicker
baby carriage in which she had tucked me
three months old to lie out in the fresh air
of my first January the carriage
was shaking she said and went on shaking
and she saw I was lying there laughing
she told me about it later it was
something that reassured her in a life
in which she had lost everyone she loved
before I was born and she had just begun
to believe that she might be able to
keep me as I lay there in the winter
laughing it was what she was thinking of
later when she told me that I had been
a happy child and she must have kept that
through the gray cloud of all her days and now
out of the horn of dreams of my own life
I wake again into the laughing child

THE OTHER HOUSE

I come back again to the old house
that I thought I knew for most of a lifetime
the house I reclaimed from abandon and ruin
and that I called my home at times when I was here
and at times when I was somewhere far from here
this time I have not come to reclaim anything
but to move nothing and to touch nothing
as though I were a ghost or here in a dream
and I know it is a dream that has no age
in this dream the same river is still here
the house is the old house and I am here in the morning
in the sunlight and the same bird is singing

THE HANDWRITING OF THE OLD

It is the tidemark of an ebbing art
a code whose sense is in another time
its message floats up through moving water
that flows from a source where there are no names
the letters have forgotten each other
they have come only once with their message
they have been waiting somewhere at a gate
without knowing what they were waiting for
then they continued their silent journey
and the landscape went on moving past them
when they stopped it took them along with it
the letters became abandoned buildings
whose doors never open and never close
untouched as places long loved in absence

WHAT CAN WE CALL IT

It is never what we thought it would be
it was never wished for when it was here
the clouds do not wish for it on their way
the nesting birds are not waiting for it
it is never on time never measured
but it has no promises to keep
it remembers but only for one time
it tells us that it has never left us
but where is it where was it where will it be
where were we where are we where will we be
each time it has taken us by surprise
and vanished before we knew what to say
but who could have taught us what to call it
it can join in our laughter and sometimes
startle us for a moment in our grief
it can be given but can never be sold
it belongs to each one of us alone
yet it is not anyone's possession
wild though it is we fear only its loss

SHADOW QUESTIONS

(for Shadow)

How can so small a body
cast such a long shadow

how can the shadow stay with us
without the body

how can so quiet a creature
still greet us after the paws have gone

FROM TIME TO TIME

It is the moment just before that we
live over and over in its only time
and then recount to those who were not there
the beginning still echoes in laughter
but resounds unrecognized every time
and never comes back to begin again
there are no words for calling after it
and when it went it left no memory
but the sound of the running sheep calling
to the evening from the darkening hill
what they are calling as they run is Wait
what each one of them is calling is Wait

A BREATH OF DAY

Last night I slept on the floor of the sea
in an unsounded part of the ocean
in the morning it was a long way up
through the dark streets of a silent country
with no language in its empty houses
until I had almost reached the surface
of a morning that I had never seen
then a breeze came to it and I began
to remember the voices of young leaves
their sound of flowing before the touch of
sunlight has found them and has summoned them
with its once and for all authority
the leaves keep whispering up into it
and by that time the sea had disappeared

WAY TO GO

Walking back alone under summer trees
long after everyone I know has gone
I remember reminding myself that
I was able to fly even while I
was flying looking down into those trees
holding the doctor's daughter in my mind
she is long gone now but later I flew
across the river to the mountain woods
where the old woman lived in her cottage
she told me she had been waiting for me
she said she had known I would be coming
our meeting itself was all that mattered
I do not remember what else she said
nor leaving and flying away again
all this way with our meeting in my mind

LIVING WITH THE NEWS

Can I get used to it day after day
a little at a time while the tide keeps
coming in faster the waves get bigger
building on each other breaking records
this is not the world that I remember
then comes the day when I open the box
that I remember packing with such care
and there is the face that I had known well
in little pieces staring up at me
it is not mentioned on the front pages
but somewhere far back near the real estate
among the things that happen every day
to someone who now happens to be me
and what can I do and who can tell me
then there is what the doctor comes to say
endless patience will never be enough
the only hope is to be the daylight

RIPE SEEDS FALLING

At home in late summer after the long
spring journeys and their echoing good-byes
at home as the year's seeds begin to fall
each one alone each in its own moment
coming in its blind hope to touch the earth
its recognition even in the dark
knowing at once the place that it has touched
the place where it belongs and came to stay
this is the place that I wanted to hear
to listen to the daylight and the dark
in this moment that has come along with me

TO WORDS IN THEIR SLEEP

Have you slept the whole summer away here
with the dogs
do you believe in waking
do you dream that you are somewhere else
do you remember what you meant to say
do you remember the sounds of voices
you once heard
do you know who you are
do you still speak the old language
are you older than you can say
you who never told the whole story
only what came to mind

AUTUMN EQUINOX

One time I was almost ready to be born
before I had begun to remember
the palms of my hands had not yet unfurled
on the one tree of the whole of darkness
the tree before waiting the hearing tree
the left hand had not yet told the right hand
This is our time our season is now
the only time and you must wake and begin
to remember and to know who you are
you will come to remember but forgetting
comes on its own and you will try to tell what cannot be
told and you will have only
the old words and will try to use them
for the first time but the beginning
has gone from the words and there is no way
now to bring it back to them again
the right hand learns but the left hand is the prophet
Pain was waiting that time with her one key
long before the first daylight had appeared

THE BLACKBOARD

The question itself has not changed
but only the depths of memory
through which it rises and now in a late
dream of childhood my father is a blackboard
that I have just erased and I am standing
with my back to it holding the old worn gray
felt eraser that we will take later
out into the school yard and will clap it
against the others that were used today
and the clapping will raise a cloud of white dust
a thin ghost that will float above us
for a moment and then will be gone
and no more rises from the old erasers
almost clean and then how had my father
come to be on the blackboard it may have been
because of what he liked to call sins
of omission which sounded impressive
and he thought would impress the congregation
and where are they now the sins of omission
where is the cloud the school yard the dream
even now I am forgetting them

CONFESSION

Oh yes
there was a stone lantern
that I coveted when I first saw it
it was not in its first life
but already ancient and waiting
in shadow and silence in a room full of dust
on a round table piled with forgotten relics
by the back road out of Aurillac
longer ago than I remember now
a stone lantern tall as a stool
faces toward each of the four seasons
unlit waiting for me
to take home that one time
it knew the whole unlit way
that I could not see
and I covet it all this time later
at the end of this September

ONE OCTOBER NIGHT

Far down the other side of the shining valley
one dog is barking like a cuckoo at the strange light
Paula my love never stirred when I
slipped out through the unlit house to look at the night
where the stars I can see and those I will never see
will not ever again be in the same places
as they are at this moment
we could do with a bit of rain but the sky
shows not a hair of cloud and the breeze
scarcely reaches us
the full moon that we claim for October
shines from above the fronds of the tall Howea
we are all here together without knowing it
flying at a speed beyond thinking
the dog has stopped barking the night is still

THE WILD GEESE

It was always for the animals that I grieved most
for the animals I had seen and for those
I had only heard of or dreamed about
or seen in cages or lying beside the road
for those forgotten and those long remembered
for the lost ones that were never found again
among people there were words we all knew
even if we did not say them and although
they were always inadequate when we said them
they were there if we wanted them when the time came
with the animals always there was only
presence as long as it was present and then
only absence suddenly and no word for it
in all the great written wisdom of China
where are the animals when were they lost
where are the ancestors who knew the way
without them all the wise words are bits of sand
twitching on the dunes where the forests
once whispered in their echoing ancient tongue
and the animals knew their way among the trees
only in the old poems does their presence survive
the gibbons call from the mountain gorges
the old words all deepen the great absence

the vastness of all that has been lost
it is still there when the poet in exile
looks up long ago hearing the voices
of wild geese far above him flying home

THE UNCOUNTED AGE

It cannot be dreamed into place beforehand
old memories have been living there
undisturbed all their lives and are as young as ever
they remember the pain of the painful time only
as they imagine battles they once read about
but the rest is as present as ever
though silent now as a dream is silent
and the faces have vanished one by one
even the eyes that once seemed unforgettable
gone like a morning gone like a breath with its day
and like all that was learned and has been forgotten
and I myself this unknowable person
student of the astronomy of spiders
have come this far with only the astrolabe
of my left palm to guide my memory

PIANIST IN THE DARK

The music is not in the keys
it has never been seen
the notes set out to find
each other
listening for their way
when they move they are the music
they have always been
waiting for
the leaves stirring in the night air
as it changes around them
the rain arrives in a slow minor
the keys sing to themselves in their dream of dancing
they make their own music
they make it again

ONLY NOW

We thought we would recall the single place
we had set out for and forget the rest
but it is the going we remember
it is the way that comes along with us
and with no one else now and the place
we set out for was not there even then
it had already been forgotten there
yet we remember the river we crossed
the stone bridge and old trees where it left us
and the small bluebird above us with its
hidden nest to which it was bringing back
what it had found where did we go from there
nothing we saw then ever had a name
and the river flowed on behind us

COWBELL

It is half a lifetime since it was
given to me years after the calling
it had been made for had gone with the cows
and the cows before them down the old lane
to the sound of that bell as children answer
to names of forebears they never knew
and about whom they knew nothing
who may have been named for others before them
only the name remaining as this cowbell brought
from the shepherd's fireplace where it was his remnant
of the days when they had been rich enough
to have a cow and he put it in my hands
saying You are from here take it take it
the sound of it will make you remember
he did not tell me that there is no question
in its sound and no place or promise
only the calling of one note at a time

DRINKING TEA IN THE SMALL HOURS

An unlabelled green from Korea
second pick from the foothills of summer
taste of distance and slight rustling of leaves
on old trees with names hard to remember
as I listen after heavy rain in the night
the taste is a hush from far away
at the very moment when I sip it
trying to make it last in the knowledge
that I will forget it in the next breath
that it will be lost when I hear the cock crow
any time now across the dark valley

WATER MUSIC

As one returned day of a week the white
canoe is here again around and under me
buoying me up in the evening sky
on the blue water of a story
in which I am part of the telling
the lake is part of it just under my hand
in this canoe that does not belong to me
but is lent to me for part of a season
never long enough and the evening light
is not mine and never long enough
the rill of waters slips past my fingertips
I listen and only I hear it going
I listen to the promises it makes
with the sound of its going from close to me
within reach now by the side of the borrowed
white canoe that is taking me
on the evening sky with the story
never long enough and the promises
made of the sound of the water leaving

THE SAME RIVER

Words never told anything about it
before or after it came and was gone
it does not need to love or to know
it is complete but never finished
it carries the weightless boat of the present
I saw it once when I was a child
my father had seen it when he was a child
and had sat by it in an empty rowboat
drawn half way up the shore and moored there
my father sat with his back to the river
holding the dry handles of the long oars
thinking that he wanted to go somewhere that
he knew nothing about and could not imagine
while the river went on flowing behind him
taking the day with it as it went
and his own father had seen the river then
when he had been a child and the paddle-wheeled
boats with the tall smokestacks came upriver
and anchored in the deep water offshore
and that rowboat went out for passengers
their luggage and the mail up from Pittsburgh
that was before the coming of the railroad
the surveyors with their instruments
measuring under the trees that he had

always known and then the barge loads
of sleepers that the men who lived there
unloaded onto mule wagons and hauled
along the right-of-way to where they would
sleep while the rails were laid between Pittsburgh
and Erie but for my grandfather
it was always the river that took him
away and brought him back to the big rock
on the far bank with the white painted letters
as tall as a man announcing RIMER
that was where my father lived until
his mother took her last children and moved
downriver to town and the white painted
letters were still there the day my father
took me to see the village one summer day
and I stood between the old house and the river
and saw just upstream from the few houses
the shining water spilling over
a dam that an old man by the road said proudly
was the first of many that were planned

STILL WATER

Clouds over the mountaintops were its ancestors
fine rain gathered in rills among the hidden crags
each vein finding its way to its own kin
joining them and gathering speed and finding its voices
taking along flakes of starlight moonlight
daylight down through the wild distances
through dreams of flying and forgetting
and dreams of belonging but departing
now it lies there at last by its green pasture
and cradles the stillness of the empty sky
this is the present it was flowing toward
this is the face that it can never see

NO TWILIGHT

How suddenly now it seems that the day
is over and on the island where I
have lived these late happy years of my life
that Paula and I have been together
there is no twilight when the day is done
the day's shadow is gone in the moment
it was here with all that went before
gone the same way into the one night
where time means nothing that is visible
when I look up after the light has gone
hearing a seed fall somewhere in the dark

THE SOUND OF FORGETTING

All night while the rain fell
the dark valley heard in silence
the silent valley did not remember
you were asleep beside me
while the rain fell all around us
I listened to you breathing
I wanted to remember
the sound of your breath
but we lay there forgetting
asleep and awake
forgetting a breath at a time
while the rain went on falling around us

HERE TOGETHER

These days I can see us clinging to each other
as we are swept along by the current
I am clinging to you to keep you from
being swept away and you are clinging to me
to keep me from being swept away from you
we see the shores blurring past as we hold
each other in the rushing current
the daylight rushes unheard far above us
how long will we be swept along in the daylight
how long will we cling together in the night
and where will it carry us together

ONE SONNET OF SUMMER

Summer has come to the trees reaching up for it
it has come in daylight without a sound
it arrived when the trees were dark in sleep
they dreamed it and woke knowing it was there
but I am an autumn child and my first
summer I was here but was not yet born
I heard the leaves whisper on their branches
and the cicadas growing in their song
I listened to all the language of summer
in which the time was talking to itself
I was born in autumn knowing the sound of summer

NO BELIEVER

Still not believing in age I wake
to find myself older than I can understand
with most of my life in a fragment
that only I remember
some of the old colors are still there
but not the voices or what they are saying
how can it be old when it is now
with the sky taking itself for granted
there was no beginning I was there

IN THE MEANTIME

Day after day this summer's rain
keeps them from setting up
our tombstone
let us stay home together my love
and not know
as the rain does not know where it came from
and the sea that is
all around us
does not know its beginning

OLD MAN AT HOME ALONE IN THE MORNING

There are questions that I no longer ask
and others that I have not asked for a long time
that I return to and dust off and discover
that I'm smiling and the question
has always been me and that it is
no question at all but that it means
different things at the same time
yes I am old now and I am the child
I remember what are called the old days and there is
no one to ask how they became the old days
and if I ask myself there is no answer
so this is old and what I have become
and the answer is something I would come to
later when I was old but this morning
is not old and I am the morning
in which the autumn leaves have no question
as the breeze passes through them and is gone

DECEMBER MORNING

How did I come to this late happiness
as I wake into my remaining days
another morning in my life with Paula
taking me by surprise like the first one
I know it is rash to speak about happiness
with the Fates so near that I can hear them
but this morning even the old regrets
seem to have lost their rancor
and to harbor shy hopes like the first grass
of spring appearing between paving stones
when I was a small child and I see
that each step has been leading me
to the present morning that I recognize
before daylight and I forget that
I am almost blind and I see the piles
of books I was going to read next
there they wait like statues of sitting dogs
faithful to someone they used to know
but happiness has a shape made of air
it was never owned by anyone
it comes when it will in its own time

UNTOLD

The taste of falling is something we
ignore but that we never forget
we do not know how many animals
we share it with or what creatures
at every moment die away from it
without ever saying a word about it
they are gone they are gone but we go on
breathing it breathing it but without
ever knowing it without ever saying it
this very moment it has come and gone
without ever having had a name
how can we address it as long as we live
why would we want to as long as we live
besides all the nothings we say
between shining and laughing
sometimes we even forget silence
but silence forgets us at every breath

VOICES OVER WATER

There are spirits that come back to us
when we have grown into another age
we recognize them just as they leave us
we remember them when we cannot hear them
some of them come from the bodies of birds
some arrive unnoticed like forgetting
they do not recall earlier lives
and there are distant voices still hoping to find us

THE PRESENT

As they were leaving the garden
one of the angels bent down to them and whispered

I am to give you this
as you are leaving the garden

I do not know what it is
or what it is for
what you will do with it

you will not be able to keep it
but you will not be able

to keep anything
yet they both reached at once

for the present
and when their hands met

they laughed

ABOUT THE AUTHOR

W.S. Merwin has published over twenty books of poetry, including *The Moon before Morning*; *The Shadow of Sirius*, which won the 2009 Pulitzer Prize; *Present Company*; and *Migration: New & Selected Poems*, which won the 2005 National Book Award. He has also published more than twenty books of translation, including *Selected Translations 1948–2011*, *Sun at Midnight* (*Poems and Letters by Musō Soseki*), *Collected Haiku of Yosa Buson*, and volumes by Federico García Lorca, Pablo Neruda, and others.

Merwin is a seven-time nominee for the National Book Award and has twice won the Pulitzer Prize for poetry. His other honors include the Lannan Literary Award for Lifetime Achievement, the Aiken Taylor Award for Modern American Poetry, the Bollingen Prize, a Ford Foundation grant, the Ruth Lilly Poetry Prize, the PEN Translation Prize, the Shelley Memorial Award, the Wallace Stevens Award, and a Lila Wallace-Reader's Digest Writers' Award, as well as fellowships from the Academy of American Poets, the Guggenheim Foundation, the National Endowment for the Arts, and the Rockefeller Foundation. In 2010, Merwin was appointed the Library of Congress's seventeenth Poet Laureate Consultant in Poetry. He currently lives and works in Hawaii.

We gratefully acknowledge the following individuals
for their support of the work of W.S. Merwin.

John Branch

David Brewster

Diana Broze

Deborah Buchanan

Sarah J. Cavanaugh

Janet & Leslie Cox

Betsey Curran

Vasiliki Dwyer

Catherine A. Edwards

Jane Ellis & Jack Litewka

Mimi Gardner Gates

Dan Gerber

Linda Fay Gerrard &
Walter Parsons

Kip Greenthal

Arthur Hanlon

Steven Holl

Maureen Lee

Jeanne Marie Lee

Jayne Lindley

Brice Marden

Ken Masters

Susan O'Connor

H. Stewart Parker

Peter T. Phinny

Joseph C. Roberts

Cynthia Sears

Rick Simonson

Dan Waggoner

Emily Warn

Jim & Mary Lou Wickwire

Charles & Barbara Wright

Poetry is vital to language and living. Since 1972, Copper Canyon Press has published extraordinary poetry from around the world to engage the imaginations and intellects of readers, writers, booksellers, librarians, teachers, students, and donors.

WE ARE GRATEFUL FOR THE MAJOR SUPPORT PROVIDED BY:

THE PAUL G. ALLEN
FAMILY FOUNDATION

amazon *literary partnership*

the point
envision·enact·evolve

4
CULTURE

golden lasso

Lannan

National Endowment for the Arts
arts.gov
ART WORKS.

A&
OFFICE OF ARTS & CULTURE
SEATTLE

WASHINGTON STATE
ARTS COMMISSION

TO LEARN MORE ABOUT UNDERWRITING
COPPER CANYON PRESS TITLES,
PLEASE CALL 360-385-4925 EXT. 103

WE ARE GRATEFUL FOR THE MAJOR SUPPORT PROVIDED BY:

Anonymous

Donna and Matt Bellew

John Branch

Diana Broze

Janet and Les Cox

Beroz Ferrell & The Point, LLC

Alan Gartenhaus and Rhoady Lee

Mimi Gardner Gates

Linda Gerrard and Walter Parsons

Gull Industries, Inc.
  on behalf of William and
  Ruth True

Mark Hamilton and Suzie Rapp

Carolyn and Robert Hedin

Steven Myron Holl

Lakeside Industries, Inc.
  on behalf of Jeanne Marie Lee

Maureen Lee and Mark Busto

Brice Marden

Ellie Mathews and Carl Youngmann
  as The North Press

H. Stewart Parker

Penny and Jerry Peabody

John Phillips and Anne O'Donnell

Joseph C. Roberts

Cynthia Lovelace Sears and
  Frank Buxton

The Seattle Foundation

Kim and Jeff Seely

David and Catherine Eaton Skinner

Dan Waggoner

C.D. Wright and Forrest Gander

Charles and Barbara Wright

The dedicated interns and
  faithful volunteers of
  Copper Canyon Press

This book is set in MVB Verdigris, a contemporary digital
typeface by Mark van Bronkhorst, inspired by Jean Jannon
and Pierre Haultin's metal types cut in sixteenth-century
France. Display type set in Garamond 3, digitized from the
1936 metal type of Morris Fuller Benton. Book design by
VJB/Scribe. Printed on archival-quality paper.

Garden Time is also issued in a signed, limited edition of
150 numbered copies and 26 lettered copies. These limited
editions are available exclusively through donation to
Copper Canyon Press.
Please e-mail gifts@coppercanyonpress.org for more details.